BATTLE OF
LITTLE
BIGHORN

BY JOHN HAMILTON

VISIT US AT
WWW.ABDOPUBLISHING.COM

Published by ABDO Publishing Company, PO Box 398166, Minneapolis, MN 55439. Copyright ©2014 by Abdo Consulting Group, Inc. International copyrights reserved in all countries. No part of this book may be reproduced in any form without written permission from the publisher. ABDO & Daughters™ is a trademark and logo of ABDO Publishing Company.

Printed in the United States of America, North Mankato, Minnesota.
122013
012014

 PRINTED ON RECYCLED PAPER

Editor: Sue Hamilton
Graphic Design: Sue Hamilton
Cover Design: Neil Klinepier
Cover Photo: Alamy
Interior Images: Alamy-pgs 17 & 29 (bottom); AP-pg 19; Corbis-pgs 1, 11, 20 & 28; History In Full Color Restoration/Colorization-pgs 10, 14, 15, & 16; Dreamstime-pg 18; Getty-pgs 22, 24, 26 & 29 (top); Harper's Weekly-pg 6; John Hamilton-pgs 13 & 21; John Mix Stanley (artist)-pg 7; Library of Congress-pgs 5, 10, 12, 15, 16 & 27 & background pgs 4-5 & 24-25; National Archives and Record Administration-pgs 8, 9 & 23; National Portrait Gallery/Smithsonian Institute-pg 14; Richard Lorenz (artist)-pg 25; Thinkstock-All backgrounds except pgs 4-5 & 24-25.

ABDO Booklinks
To learn more about Great Battles, visit ABDO Publishing Company online. Web sites about Great Battles are featured on our Booklinks pages. These links are routinely monitored and updated to provide the most current information available. Web site: www.abdopublishing.com

Library of Congress Control Number: 2013946974

Cataloging-in-Publication Data

Hamilton, John, 1959-
 Battle of Little Bighorn / John Hamilton.
   p. cm. -- (Great battles)
Includes index.
ISBN 978-1-62403-205-9
1. Little Bighorn, Battle of the, Mont., 1876--Juvenile literature.   I. Title.
973.8/2--dc23

2013946974

CONTENTS

A CLASH OF TWO
CULTURES

Lieutenant Colonel George Armstrong Custer, battalion commander of the U.S. Army's 7th Cavalry, stood on a bluff overlooking the Little Bighorn River, in south-central Montana. He couldn't believe his eyes. Spread out on the valley bottom were hundreds of teepees. It was the biggest Native American camp Custer or any of his men had ever seen.

The golden-haired cavalry leader's luck had come through once again. He had caught his foe, Lakota Chief Sitting Bull and his followers, in a surprise attack. The soldiers rode forward, certain of glorious victory. Within hours, however, Custer and more than a third of the men under his command would be dead.

On June 25-26, 1876, the Battle of Little Bighorn was fought between soldiers of the 7th Cavalry and warriors of the Lakota (Sioux), Northern Cheyenne, and Arapaho tribes. It was a clash between two cultures, one expanding its wealth and power, and the other fighting for its very existence.

For the Native Americans, the Battle of the Greasy Grass (as they called the Little Bighorn) was a great victory in their struggle for freedom and independence. But it also marked the beginning of the end of their way of life. Within a year after the battle, many of the participants were either on reservations or on the run. In many ways, the Battle of Little Bighorn was Sitting Bull's, not Custer's, last stand.

Native American warriors circle around the United States Army's 7th Cavalry soldiers during the Battle of Little Bighorn on June 25, 1876.

KEY EVENTS BEFORE THE
BATTLE

The Battle of Little Bighorn was part of a larger conflict called the Great Sioux War of 1876, which lasted about one year. The conflict had been brewing for a long time. For hundreds of years, ever since Europeans settled in North America, there had been cultural friction between the newcomers and the Native Americans. Mostly, they fought over land.

During the 1800s, citizens of the United States pushed into the interior of the continent. They believed they had a "manifest destiny," a God-given right to expand "from sea to shining sea." To them, America was a limitless land that was theirs for the taking. They wanted land, timber, farms, and minerals, especially gold. There was one thing standing in their way: the millions of people who already called the land their home—the Native Americans.

Native Americans observe a large wagon train of settlers.

Plains Indians on a buffalo hunt in the 1800s.

The Indians of the Northern Plains lived off the land, and they were perhaps the most free people on Earth. Ever since horses were introduced to their culture in the 1600s, the Plains Indians were free to live wherever they wanted. They followed migrating herds of animals, such as the American bison (commonly called buffalo). European-Americans wanted the Indians to become peaceful farmers, but the Native Americans were hunters and warriors. It was their way of life, and they were not about to change voluntarily.

The Treaty of Fort Laramie was signed in April 1868.

Although the Plains Indians resisted change, by the mid-1800s many tribal leaders realized that the expansion of white society was an unstoppable force. The invaders of their land were too technologically advanced, and there were far too many of them. Many Lakota, Dakota, and Arapaho chiefs signed the 1868 Treaty of Fort Laramie. The agreement set aside large sections of land in present-day western South Dakota. The Native Americans agreed to live on these reservations and give up their nomadic lifestyle. In exchange, the government promised to provide food, schooling, and other support. The American government hoped that putting the Plains Indians on reservations would stop conflicts with other tribes and white settlers.

Many Indian leaders, such as Sitting Bull and Crazy Horse, refused to sign the treaty. They rejected the reservations because they didn't want to be forced to stay in one place. They also didn't want to depend on the American government, which had broken treaties in the past. These Indians were also joined by those who had signed the treaty, but ventured off the reservation during the summer months to hunt migrating herds of buffalo. As the government feared, they were soon fighting with enemy tribes and settlers.

In 1874, Lieutenant Colonel George Armstrong Custer led an expedition into the Black Hills of South Dakota. They were scouting for a place to build a fort to monitor the Native American tribes, but they were also looking for something more valuable. Geologists soon confirmed a long-standing rumor: there were vast quantities of gold buried in the Black Hills.

When the news of Custer's expedition was made public, prospectors began pouring into the Black Hills by the thousands. Bustling mining towns such as Deadwood, South Dakota, soon sprang to life. But there was a big problem: all these white treasure hunters were trespassers, the equivalent of illegal aliens. The Black Hills had been given to the Native Americans as part of the 1868 Treaty of Fort Laramie. The gold seekers had no legal right to be there.

The year before gold was discovered in the Black Hills, the United States was gripped by a deep economic recession. The Panic of 1873 caused many hardships, including 20 percent unemployment. President Ulysses S. Grant needed to find an economic stimulus for the ailing economy, and the promise of new gold was a good solution. Gold would create jobs and replenish the U.S. Treasury.

Lieutenant Colonel George Custer leads an 1874 expedition across the plains of the Dakota Territory.

The United States offered the Native Americans about $7 million for their land. But the Black Hills, known as *Paha Sapa* to the Lakota, were sacred ground to the Native Americans. How, they argued, could they sell the land that their ancestors had walked upon? In addition, tribal leaders such as Sitting Bull feared that if they sold the Black Hills, the tribes would be selling their own

future. The government's offer was soundly rejected.

President Grant had a difficult choice to make. Many people thought the government should honor its treaty commitments to the Native Americans. But by now there were an estimated 15,000 whites living in the Black Hills, far too many to arrest and deport. Plus, the government badly wanted the area's gold deposits.

U.S. President Ulysses S. Grant

It was also fed up with attacks on white settlers and the railroads.

President Grant met with his advisors in November 1875, including Generals Philip Sheridan and George Crook, both Civil War veterans. The decision was made to wage war on the Plains Indians.

In the spring and summer of 1876, thousands of Native Americans traveled to Sitting Bull's camp by the banks of the Little Bighorn River. They were prepared for war against the United States Army.

The Native Americans were told to get out of the Black Hills and to leave the open areas of Montana and Wyoming where the herds of buffalo roamed. The government warned that any Indians that did not move to the reservations by January 31, 1876, would be considered "hostile" to the United States. The Army would make them move to the reservations by force, if necessary.

Sitting Bull, Crazy Horse, and other tribal leaders urged their people not to go back to the reservations. It would be like living as slaves to the whites, Sitting Bull said. By the early summer of 1876, thousands of Native Americans had streamed off the reservations to join Sitting Bull at his camp in southern Montana by the banks of the Little Bighorn River. The stage was set for war.

SHERIDAN'S PLAN OF
ATTACK

In 1876, General Philip Sheridan was the commander of U.S. Army forces for much of the West. He was a Civil War veteran who learned how effective the scorched earth tactics of total war could be. Sheridan planned to use this same strategy against the Native Americans who had defied the U.S. government's order to return to their reservations.

Sheridan's plan included three large groups of soldiers who would seek out the "hostile" Indians. The soldiers would set out from different locations and hopefully corner the

General Philip Sheridan

Native tribes on the plains of Wyoming and Montana. One Army group marched eastward from Fort Ellis, in Bozeman, Montana. Another moved up from the south, from central Wyoming's Fort Fetterman. The last group was commanded by General Alfred Terry. It left from Fort Abraham Lincoln, near present-day Bismarck, North Dakota. Terry's group included a large number of soldiers from the Army's 7th Cavalry, under the command of Lieutenant Colonel George Armstrong Custer.

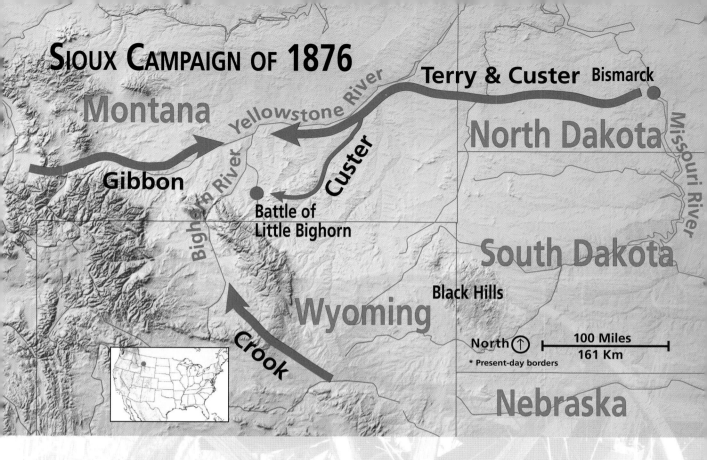

SIOUX CAMPAIGN OF 1876

Terry & Custer   Bismarck

Montana

Yellowstone River

North Dakota

Missouri River

Gibbon

Bighorn River

Custer

Battle of
Little Bighorn

South Dakota

Black Hills

Wyoming

North ⬆   100 Miles
161 Km
* Present-day borders

Crook

Nebraska

Nobody was sure exactly where the Native Americans were camped. The nomadic tribes moved often. But the Army knew the Indians usually gathered near the hunting grounds of the Yellowstone, Powder, and Little Bighorn Rivers.

General Terry's troops moved westward along the Yellowstone River in Montana. On June 22, 1876, Custer and his troops on horseback separated from Terry's group. They swiftly moved south, following Rosebud Creek. Eventually they turned west, toward the Little Bighorn River, where they strongly suspected they would find Sitting Bull's forces.

Custer's mission was to attack from the south while General Terry's remaining force, combined with the troops from Fort Ellis, blocked the Indian's escape route to the north. Custer's fast cavalry troops would make sure that Sitting Bull and his warriors couldn't slip away. If all went as planned, they would take the Native Americans totally by surprise.

GEORGE ARMSTRONG CUSTER

Lieutenant Colonel George Armstrong Custer (1839-1876) was a U.S. Army 7th Cavalry commander and a key figure at the Battle of Little Bighorn. Custer graduated in 1861 from the U.S. Military Academy at West Point, New York. Self confidant to the point of arrogance, he was last in his class, more because of demerits than bad grades. Custer found fame during the Civil War (1861-1865), rising to the rank of brigadier general of U.S. Volunteers in 1863, at just 23 years old.

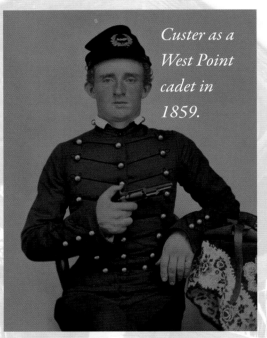

Custer as a West Point cadet in 1859.

Hailed as the "boy general," Custer earned a reputation as a daring and courageous cavalry commander. He was also reckless, fearless, strict, and vain, especially regarding his curly blond hair, which fell to his shoulders. Yet, thousands of his men loved him. He always led them personally into bloody battle. He fought 32 major engagements in the Civil War without injury, despite having 11 horses shot out from under him. Custer became a war hero and a celebrity in the press.

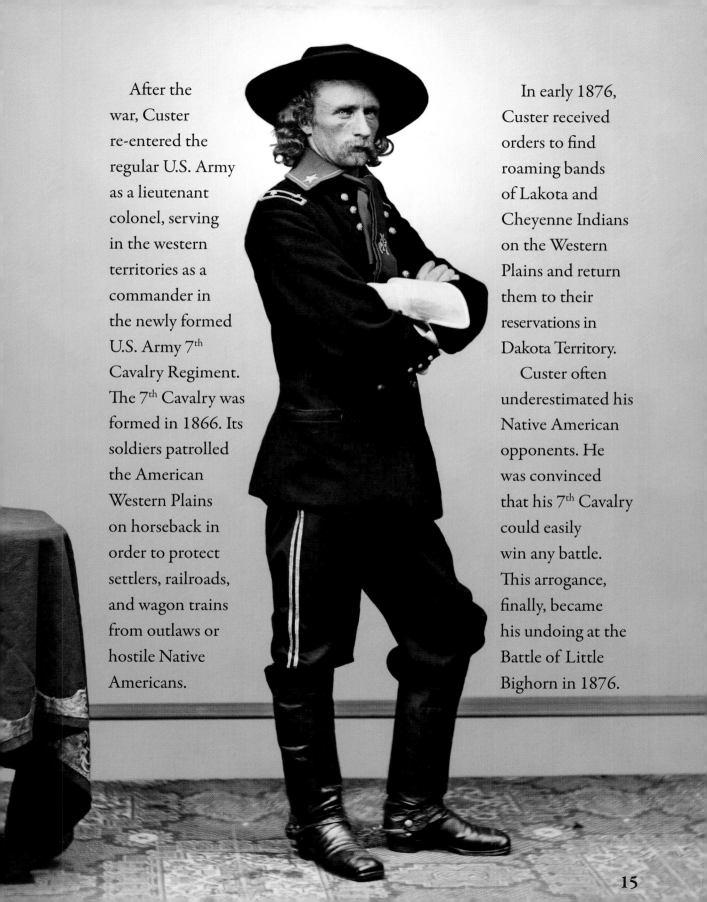

After the war, Custer re-entered the regular U.S. Army as a lieutenant colonel, serving in the western territories as a commander in the newly formed U.S. Army 7th Cavalry Regiment. The 7th Cavalry was formed in 1866. Its soldiers patrolled the American Western Plains on horseback in order to protect settlers, railroads, and wagon trains from outlaws or hostile Native Americans.

In early 1876, Custer received orders to find roaming bands of Lakota and Cheyenne Indians on the Western Plains and return them to their reservations in Dakota Territory.

Custer often underestimated his Native American opponents. He was convinced that his 7th Cavalry could easily win any battle. This arrogance, finally, became his undoing at the Battle of Little Bighorn in 1876.

PEOPLE OF THE NATIVE TRIBES

Most historians estimate that on June 25, 1876, there were at least 8,000 Native Americans camped along the banks of the Little Bighorn River in south-central Montana. Of these, between 1,500 and 2,000 were warriors.

Chief Sitting Bull

The people of the camp were mainly Lakota (Sioux), Northern Cheyenne, and Arapaho Indians. The Lakota were the most powerful tribe on the plains. One of their leaders was **Sitting Bull** (1831-1890). He was a member of the Hunkpapa Lakota tribe. In his youth, Sitting Bull was a skilled and brave warrior who fought in many battles. He became a holy man who guided his people. He especially resisted attempts by the U.S. government to restrict Native Americans to reservations. Before the Battle of Little Bighorn, Sitting Bull had a vision in which he foresaw the defeat of the U.S. 7th Cavalry. Although he didn't fight at the Battle of Little Bighorn, he rallied his people to victory.

After the battle, Sitting Bull fled with a group of Lakota to Canada. In 1881, he returned to the United States and surrendered to military authorities. He toured briefly with Buffalo Bill Cody's Wild West. In 1890, he was shot and killed during a struggle with police on the Standing Rock Indian Reservation in South Dakota.

Crazy Horse (1840-1877) was one of the greatest Native American warriors in history. A member of the Oglala Lakota tribe, he took part in many battles on the Western Plains. He was fearless and clever. He once had a vision which made him believe he was invincible against enemy weapons. He applied body paint before battle that resembled hailstones. Down the right side of his face he drew a red lightning strike. His acts of bravery were legendary.

During the Battle of Little Bighorn, Crazy Horse rode his horse directly in front of the white soldiers, drawing their fire. After the battle, Crazy Horse continued to resist the U.S. government's attempt to put his people on reservations. Finally, in May 1877, Crazy Horse surrendered, along with 1,100 followers. That autumn, he was stabbed to death during a fight with a guard.

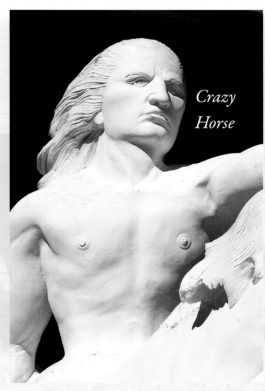

Crazy Horse

TACTICS AND WEAPONS

During the Battle of Little Bighorn, the troops of the 7th Cavalry were issued 1873 Trapdoor .45/70-cartridge Springfield carbines. The large, .45-caliber cartridges were loaded by swinging up a "trapdoor" on the breech (rear) of the barrel. Carbines have a shorter barrel than regular rifles, which make them easier to carry and shoot on horseback. The 1873 Springfield was highly reliable and packed a terrific punch. Its major weakness was that it had to be reloaded after each shot, meaning a skilled trooper could shoot only about 10 rounds per minute. The U.S. Army compensated for this by training soldiers to dismount and fire in "skirmish lines," with each man standing or kneeling about five yards (4.6 m) apart in a line. This organized firing method worked well against enemy charges. Soldiers could fire simultaneously, or they could shoot "at will" as the battle progressed.

Soldiers of the 7th Cavalry were also armed with Model 1873 Colt Single-Action Army .45-caliber revolvers. Famous as "the gun that won the West," the Colt .45 could fire up to six rounds before reloading.

Colt .45

Springfield Carbine

Traditional Native American clubs were an effective weapon at close range.

Winchester Model 1866

The Native Americans used a variety of weapons at Little Bighorn. Many carried the Winchester Model 1866 lever-action repeating rifle, which fired .44-caliber rimfire cartridges. At close range, the Winchester was far superior to the U.S. Army's Springfield carbine. It could be fired as fast as a person could work the lever and pull the trigger, and it could shoot 13 rounds at a time without reloading.

Many other kinds of firearms were used by the Native Americans, including those manufactured by Remington, Sharps, and Colt. The Indians also used bows and arrows, lances, clubs, and knives. These traditional weapons were simple, yet brutally effective at close range, especially in the hands of skilled warriors.

RENO'S
CHARGE

On the morning of June 25, 1876, George Armstrong Custer's Crow and Arikara Indian scouts informed the lieutenant colonel

A reenactment of the 7th Cavalry's charge at the Battle of Little Bighorn on June 25, 1876.

that they had found Sitting Bull's camp of Native Americans. Nestled along the shores of the Little Bighorn River, the camp was the largest the scouts had ever seen. Hundreds of teepees housed at least 8,000 Lakota, Northern Cheyenne, and Arapaho Indians. The scouts warned Custer that the 7th Cavalry didn't have enough bullets to fight all those people.

Custer, in his usual headstrong way, decided to attack the village immediately, refusing to wait for reinforcements. His years as a cavalry commander had taught him that he could fight his way out of almost any scrap. He was confident that he could defeat any band of mere "savages." Also, Custer didn't want the Indians to detect the 7th Cavalry's presence, scatter into small groups, and escape. He wanted to capture them all at once so that he could force them back to the reservation in one large group.

Battle of Little Bighorn

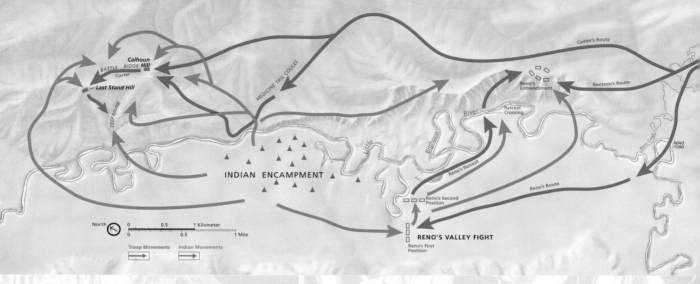

The 7th Cavalry was on a bluff overlooking the Little Bighorn River, which flowed to the north. The village was across the river, to the west. The men's view of the Indian camp was limited because of the twists and turns in the river. Ridges along the bluffs also blocked their line of sight.

Custer threw caution to the wind and sent a group of 120 men, commanded by Captain Frederick Benteen, to the south. They were ordered to scout and cut off any possible Indian retreat. Custer then ordered Major Marcus Reno, with a group of 140 men, to cross the river on horseback and charge down the valley toward the camp.

Custer personally commanded a group of about 210 men and moved north along the bluffs. His plan was to swing wide and attack the village from the north, hopefully taking groups of fleeing women and children hostage in order to convince the enemy to surrender. This two-pronged attack was a tactic that Custer had used successfully in the past against Native Americans.

Down in the village, Native Americans were going about their daily chores. Children played in the river. Suddenly, a cry went up. "White warriors are coming!" In the face of Major Reno's thunderous cavalry charge, women and children fled to the north in terror. Sitting Bull rallied his people, encouraging his young warriors to prepare for battle. Oglala Lakota Chief Low Dog said he was surprised anyone would attack the camp, since they were so strong in numbers. "The soldiers came on us like thunderbolts," he said.

As Major Reno rounded a bend in the valley, he got his first full glimpse of the immensity of the Indian camp. It was obvious to him that Custer had vastly underestimated its size. Just before reaching the edge of the village, Reno halted the cavalry charge. He ordered his men to dismount and form a protective skirmish line. Two soldiers were unable to stop their horses and rode right into the village. They were never seen alive again. The soldiers began firing their Springfield rifles into the camp.

Chief Gall

Within minutes, about 600 Indian warriors counterattacked. Many of them were on horseback. Hunkpapa Lakota Chief Gall's two wives and three daughters were killed in Reno's opening attack. "My heart was very bad that day," Gall said. He was so angry he threw his weapons down and rushed into battle with his bare hands.

Major Reno knew he was greatly outnumbered. His men dropped back into a stand of woods near the riverbank. He screamed a question to his scout, Bloody Knife. The scout was hit by a bullet to the head. Gore sprayed all over Reno, sending the major into a panic. "Those who want to escape, follow me!" he cried out. The men withdrew across the river and up the east bank toward the safety of high ground.

Dozens of troopers were killed during the rout. It was every man for himself. Cheyenne Chief Two Moons said it was like a buffalo hunt. Warriors raced next to the soldiers and shot at them or beat them with clubs. The river ran red with blood.

Finally, Reno and the other survivors made it to the top of the ridge. By chance, they met Captain Benteen and his group. Benteen was responding to a note from Custer. The lieutenant colonel, after realizing the full extent of the Indian camp, had ordered Benteen to reinforce his position. "Benteen," the note said. "Come on. Big village. Be quick. Bring packs…"

Reno begged Benteen to stay and help his wounded and exhausted men. To the north, they heard the distant sound of gunshots. They knew it was Custer. Their commanding officer was in trouble. Some men made an attempt to reach Custer, but they were turned back by gathering Indian warriors. All they could do now was dig in and fight for their lives.

LAST
STAND

Not a single soldier under George Armstrong Custer's immediate command survived the Battle of Little Bighorn. Nobody knows for sure what happened during "Custer's Last Stand," but Native American eyewitnesses and archeological evidence give us clues.

Custer and his men may have descended the bluffs and tried to cross the Little Bighorn River, but were repelled by Indian sharpshooters. They moved back uphill to safer ground. They found their way blocked by more than 1,500 Native Americans, all in hot pursuit of the men of the 7th Cavalry.

Custer and his men were surrounded by thousands of Native American warriors.

Not a single soldier under Custer's immediate command survived the Battle of Little Bighorn.

Custer was no longer attacking. He had become the hunted. Native Americans took cover in the ravines and gullies, popping up to fire at the surrounded soldiers with rifles or arrows. Much of the fighting became hand-to-hand combat. Custer's men fought for their lives, but were eventually shot or clubbed to death. Some soldiers killed their horses and hid behind them. The Indians fired arrows high into the air so that they rained down on the men behind the horses. The soldiers were running out of ammo as the Indians came closer and closer. Some men panicked and ran to a nearby ravine, where they were all hunted down.

At one point, at what today is called Last Stand Hill, Custer himself was shot and killed.

There may not have even been a heroic "last stand," like the kind seen in Hollywood movies. The soldiers may simply have been overrun in a massive Indian charge. Cheyenne Chief Two Moons later said, "We swirled around the soldiers like water around a stone."

It was all over very quickly. Chief Gall said the fight lasted "about as long as it takes for a hungry man to eat his dinner." The gunfire became more and more spaced out, and then finally stopped. For Custer and his men, the battle was over.

THE BATTLE'S
AFTERMATH

On their hilltop fortification south of Custer's fateful battle, Captain Benteen and his men fought hard against the Native American warriors. The soldiers dug pits in the ground with spoons, cups, knives, even their bare hands, to protect themselves against Indian bullets and arrows. They were besieged for almost an entire day. At last, on June 26, General Terry's army was spotted approaching from the north. The Native Americans packed up their village and fled the area. Benteen's hilltop stand had saved almost 350 soldiers.

After the Battle of Little Bighorn, Native Americans packed up their village and fled the area.

Native American chiefs gathered with military leaders in 1891. After the Battle of Little Bighorn in June 1876, their lives changed forever.

Benteen and the other survivors were horrified when they later discovered the bodies of Lieutenant Colonel Custer and their other fallen comrades. The bodies had been stripped and mutilated, partly out of Lakota ritual, and partly as revenge for earlier massacres committed by U.S. soldiers. In total, about 270 members of the 7th Cavalry had been killed, and another 55 were wounded. Between 60 and 100 Native American warriors died, possibly more.

At the Battle of the Greasy Grass, the Lakota, Cheyenne, and Arapaho people had just won their greatest victory in the struggle to keep their way of life. Their triumph, however, did not last long. Back East, news of Custer's death caused shock waves. General Sheridan was given more soldiers to patrol the West. The Plains Indians's biggest resource, the buffalo, were hunted almost to extinction.

Within a year after the battle, most Lakota and Cheyenne were disarmed and confined to reservations. In addition, the Black Hills were taken by the U.S. government without payment, a wound that has not healed to this day.

A MESSAGE FOR THE
LIVING

In south-central Montana, just off Interstate 90 about 65 miles (105 km) from Billings, Montana, the United States National Park Service oversees Little Bighorn Battlefield National Monument. In 1876, the area was the scene of warfare and carnage. Today, it is hallowed ground, a peaceful place for people to learn and reflect.

The park preserves the battlefield, and also serves as a memorial to the people who fought and died there. It is the only battlefield in the country with white stone markers representing where soldiers fell in battle. There are also 17 red stone markers that show where Native Americans died. (Many more Indians died at the battle,

Markers for Custer and other soldiers.

A marker for a Sioux warrior.

Headstones mark where Custer and his men fell on Last Stand Hill.

but these 17 are confirmed by family oral histories.) George Armstrong Custer's marker shows where he died on Last Stand Hill, along with many of his comrades.

Also on Last Stand Hill are two memorials. A large stone marker commemorates soldiers of the U.S. Army's 7th Cavalry who died on the battlefield. It was placed in 1881. In 2003, the "Peace Through Unity" Indian Memorial was dedicated to honor Native American men, women, and children who died on the sacred ground defending their way of life. The memorial was built to "encourage peace among all the races."

Spirit Warriors Sculpture at the "Peace Through Unity" Indian Memorial.

GLOSSARY

BATTALION

A group of a large number of soldiers ready for battle. A battalion's size ranges from several hundred to 1,200. It is usually commanded by a lieutenant colonel.

BISON

Also called the American buffalo, bison are large bovines, like cattle or oxen. They have shaggy brown hair, short legs, and horns. They are massive creatures. Fully grown males can weigh over 2,000 pounds (907 kg). Bison were very important to the nomadic Plains Indians, which used the animals for food, clothing, rope, teepee coverings, and many other uses.

CARBINE

A rifle with a short barrel. They are usually easier to handle than normal long-barreled rifles. Carbines were the preferred weapon of cavalry troops.

CAVALRY

Military units in which soldiers fought on horseback. Cavalry units were highly mobile. They could move much faster and farther than infantry troops. Massed cavalry charges were highly effective against enemies on foot.

CIVIL WAR

A war where two parts of the same nation fight against each other. The American Civil War was fought between Northern and Southern states from 1861–1865. The Southern states were for slavery. They wanted to start their own country. Northern states fought against slavery and a division of the country.

DAKOTA TERRITORY

A territory of the United States, formed in 1861, that later was split and became the states of North and South Dakota.

PLAINS INDIANS

Tribes of Native Americans who live on the Great Plains of the United States and Canada. Before being displaced by white settlers, the tribes roamed the land on horseback, hunting great herds of buffalo and other migrating animals for subsistence. Plains Indian tribes included the Lakota, Cheyenne, and Arapaho, all of whom fought at the Battle of Little Bighorn.

RESERVATION

Areas of land set aside for Native American tribes. There are over 300 Indian reservations in the United States. People living on reservations have their own tribal governments and laws, which can differ from the laws of the lands surrounding them.

SCOUT

A member of a military unit that moves ahead of the main group to gather information about the enemy or countryside. Crow and Arikara Indians were employed by the U.S. Army's 7th Cavalry as scouts. They were enemies of the Lakota, and well acquainted with the Plains. They led Custer and the 7th Cavalry to the Lakota camp at the Little Bighorn.

SIOUX

Another name for Lakota or Dakota Native Americans.

TEEPEE

A Native American dwelling used especially by the Plains Indians such as the Lakota or Cheyenne. Teepees are conical in shape, made of animal hide or cloth, with frames made of long wooden poles.

TOTAL WAR

A class of warfare in which there is no difference made between soldiers and civilians. The entire resources of a people, including military bases and cities, are considered hostile and can be freely attacked.

INDEX